HE FINAL WORD ON MiC DROPPiN

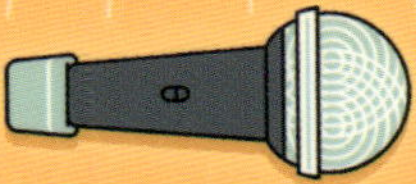

THE FINAL WORD ON MIC DROPPIN'

WRITTEN BY
Donald Lemke

ILLUSTRATED BY
Jord O'Brien

RP MINIS
PHILADELPHIA

RP Minis®
Hachette Book Group
1290 Avenue of the Americas, New York, NY 10104
www.runningpress.com
@Running_Press

First Edition: October 2025

Published by RP Minis, an imprint of Hachette Book Group, Inc. The RP Minis name and logo is a registered trademark of Hachette Book Group, Inc.

Contact specialmarkets@hbgusa.com regarding special discounts for bulk purchases.

The publisher is not responsible for websites (or their content) that are not owned by the publisher.

Design by Amanda Richmond

ISBN: 979-8-89414-133-6

Made in Dongguan, China (HKD) 06/25 #01

"Peace out."

drops mic

—Some Guy,
leaving on a high note

INTRODUCTION

We've all been there . . . You've just said something profound, nailed a joke, or—let's be totally honest—survived a years-long workweek. And in that oh-so-glorious moment, you wished that you had a microphone to drop. With its infamous *KLUNK* and high-pitched feedback squeal, you know a mic drop is an epic punctuation (an exclamation, even) to any well-timed statement. The perfect way of saying (without saying anything at all), "That's right, folks. I *am* really that good."

Well, my sometimes-petty friends, wish no more!

Whether you've just closed out a meeting with a killer PP presentation, put the final touches on an all-nighter project, or simply walked out of work on a Friday (Can I get a "TGIF!"), this mini marvel is here to seal the deal.

But don't be fooled—this isn't any ordinary desk toy. The *Mini Mic Drop* is your secret weapon for life's victories, both big and small. Think of it as a standing ovation on demand. Every time you let it drop, that satisfying sound (and maybe even some applause) will remind the world just how awesome you are.

From crushing deadlines to delivering iconic comebacks, the *Mini Mic Drop* is here for all your mic-drop-worthy moments. So get ready, take a bow, and leave them utterly speechless—because if you're dropping the mic, you've already won.

MIC-DROP-WORTHY MOMENTS

To be honest, you're not the first to dream of droppin' the mic. The annals of history are filled with individuals who *should* have dropped a mic. (Also, mic drop for using *annals* in a sentence.) Let's take a look at some of the greatest mic-drop-worthy moments the world has never known:

1. Trojan Horse? More Like Trojan Force!

12th Century BC—After sneaking out of the infamous Trojan Horse, Greek soldiers launched their surprise attack on Troy.

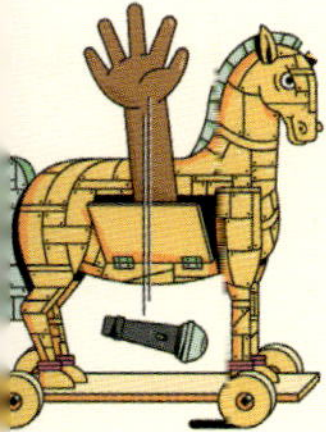

Once the city was theirs, if they had a mic (or, you know, some kind of ancient voice amplifier), they would've dropped it right there on the battlefield with a smug, "Thanks for the hospitality, suckers!" before riding off into the sunset.

2. #Rug Life

31 BC—Cleopatra (aka, the ultimate Girl Boss) knew how to make an entrance. When she met Mark Antony, sparks flew—but let's talk about that rug move. Yes, Cleopatra literally rolled herself up and had servants deliver her like an overnight Amazon package. As she dramatically unrolled and stood up, there should've been a mic in her hand, ready to drop. If there was ever a "drop and walk away" moment, that was it. Though let's be real: Cleo probably struck a royal pose first.

3. We the People . . . Are Out!

July 4, 1776—Ye olde Tommy Jefferson handed his freshly signed Declaration of

Independence to his white-wigged compatriots. And if mics had existed back then (FYI: They didn't), it would've hit the floor with a *THUNK* so loud it might have echoed all the way to King George's bedchamber. #MicDrop #WeDaPeeps

4. That's Relatively Genius

1905—Albert Einstein scribbled down the theory of relativity ($e=mc^2$), looked at the chalkboard, and thought, “I think we’re done here.” If only he had a mini mic to drop . . . (Question: If a mic travels at the speed of sound, does it bend space-time? The world may never know.)

5. BOOM to the Moon

July 20, 1969—After stepping onto the moon, Neil Armstrong delivered his iconic line, “One small step for man, one giant leap for mankind.” If ever there was a moment to drop a mic in zero gravity, this was it. (Though, considering the whole "vacuum of space" thing, maybe a virtual mic drop would've been more practical . . . or at least less floaty.)

DROP IT LIKE IT'S HOT

Not sure when to unleash the power of the *Mini Mic Drop*? Don't worry, we've got you covered. Here are some prime-time opportunities to make your statement and let the mic fall (with appropriate flair, of course):

1. Nailed It at Work

You've just given the perfect

presentation (PP slides were flawless, of course) or solved a problem your coworkers have been puzzling over for days. *That* is a mic-drop moment, my friend. Grab your *Mini Mic Drop*, let it fall gently onto the conference table, and bask in your moment of office glory.

2. The Last Word in an Argument

You've been trading jabs back and forth, but finally—*finally*—you land the ultimate comeback. No need to say more. Drop that mic and walk away (preferably in dramatic sloOOOoOoo-mOOOoooO).

3. Survived a Monday

Sometimes, just getting through the day feels like a victory worthy of applause (a standing O, even). Made it to the end of Monday without losing your mind? That's a mic-drop moment if we've ever heard one. Time to celebrate with a satisfying *THUNK* of the *Mini Mic Drop*.

4. Weekend Victories

You cleaned your entire apartment. You ran errands. You resisted the urge to nap for three hours (settling for *two* instead). When you've conquered the weekend, it's time for a mic drop—preferably before collapsing onto the couch in triumph.

5. Winning at Family Game Night

You've just demolished your five-year-old in Monopoly, and there's only one thing left to do. Drop that mic. But be gentle—those family bonds are fragile, after all.

6. Epic Burn in a Group Chat

We all have that one friend who *thinks* they're the funniest person in the group chat. (Hint: It's probably you, amirite?) When you finally deliver that epic burn, it's time to back up your words with a mic drop. Sure, no one will hear it, but you can always send out a #micdrop follow-up.

7. Leaving Work on a Friday Afternoon

The clock strikes five-ish, your desk is (miraculously) clear, and it's officially the weekend. That's the kind of freedom that deserves a mic drop before you head for the door like you're escaping Shawshank. Bonus points if you can nail it while walking backward in sunglasses. (EXTRA bonus points if you can do it without tripping. . . .)

DROP IT LIKE A PRO

While dropping the mic may seem effortless, there's a subtle art to it. You want to strike the perfect balance of dramatic flair and cool nonchalance. Follow these steps, and you'll be mic-droppin' like a pro in no time flat:

PAUSE FOR EFFECT

Before you drop the mic, give it a beat. Let the room (or, you know, your *cat*) feel the weight of your brilliance. Silence is golden—right before the mic hits the floor.

DROP IT (DON'T THROW IT)

This is a *drop*, not a launch. Let gravity do its thing. Hold the mini mic loosely and let it fall naturally. (We're going for finesse, not force, after all.)

THE WALK-OFF

The key to any successful mic drop is the exit. After you drop the mic, don't stick around waiting for validation. Turn and walk away like the hero you are (but maybe peek over your shoulder to catch the applause/confusion).

ADVANCED TECHNIQUES

THE SPIN DROP

Before you drop the mic, give it a little spin in your hand. This move adds extra flair, making the final drop even more satisfying.

(**WARNING**: Only for seasoned mic droppers. Practice on a soft surface first.)

THE DOUBLE DROP

Got two mics? (Of course, you do.) Drop them both at once to double the drama. Whether you're wrapping up a dual presentation or just feeling *extra*, the double mic drop is sure to leave an impact. (Plus, more noise.)

HOLD THE MIC

With great mic-dropping power comes great responsibility. Here's when *not* to drop the mic:

Mid-sentence: Dropping the mic halfway through a conversation? You're just confusing people, amateur.

At weddings: This is their moment, not yours. Let the

couple shine. (Unless you're the Best Man/Maid of Honor. . . . Then you're A-OK to give a highly inappropriate speech, drop the mic, and leave Grandma shaking her blue-haired head.)

During important phone calls: Your boss is on the other end? Maybe hold off on that mic drop (unless you're prepared for the consequences).

NAILED IT

Life is full of little victories, moments when you just *nail it*. And what better way to celebrate those moments than with a mic drop? With your *Mini Mic Drop*, you're equipped to own the room—whether it's your living room, boardroom, or any room in between. Just remember: Drop responsibly, bask in the applause, and keep slaying those everyday moments.

Because if you're not dropping the mic, did it even really happen? Peace out.